The Stone in my Shoe

Lucy Logsdon

Copyright © 2024 • All Rights Reserved
Pierian Springs Press
Lucy Logsdon

Other than review quotes or academic excerpts,
no part of this work may be reproduced
without explicit permission.

First Edition, October 2024
ISBN 978-1-953136-70-1 Hardback

Cover Graphic Design & Book Typography by Kurt Lovelace.
Cover artwork by Pierian Springs Press.
Cover type *Bauhaus Dessau* **Alfarn** by Céline Hurka,
Elia Preuss, Flavia Zimbardi,
Hidetaka Yamasaki, and Luca Pellegrini.
Author name, blurbs, footers in **Jenson** by Robert Slimbach.
Back cover description in **Gill Sans Nova.**
Titles and body text set in **Baskerville.**
Flourishes set in Emigre Foundry **Dalliance** by Frank Heine.
Emigre Foundry **ZeitGuys** by Bob Aufuldish, Eric Donelan.
Typefaces licensed Adobe, Linotype, Emigre, & URW GmbH.

PSPress.Pub
Pierian Springs Press, Inc
30 N Gould St, Ste 25398
Sheridan, Wyoming 82801-6317

"I am myself, but a new construction," Lucy Logsdon writes in this deep, forthright, and firmly constructed book of changes, of loss and self-definition, of grief and resurgence. THE STONE IN MY SHOE is a courageous, high-stake, unflinching book of salvations.

Edward Hirsch

Contents

Something's Broken	1
Twisted	2
Love Letter to My Surgeon	4
The Hour of the Raccoon	7
The Good, Good Cripple	8
My Last Poem	10
The Burning Girl	12
The Princess and the Pea	14
The Winter of the Duck	15
Churchill	16
Self-portrait/Burn	18
The Worrying Hour	20
Grading on a Late Winter Day	22
A Bargaining with my Forest's Fox	24
After My Banishment	26
The Bad Girl	28
Little Red 2.0	30
The Feral Child	32

Childhood of the Storyteller ... 34
How to Save Your Self ... 36
Beating the Boundaries ... 38
Envelope ... 39
Those That Come Back ... 40
Days of 1979 ... 42
Mirror, Mirror ... 44
How to Leave Yourself ... 46
Vow Vigilance ... 49
Fairytale ... 50
My Place in Line ... 52
Broken Things ... 54
In Reseda ... 56
The Good Girl ... 58
Recipe for Disaster ... 60
The Becoming ... 62
To Bring or To Not Bring Your Phone ... 64
Stepdaughter ... 66

 Acknowledgments   69

 About the Author   71

The STONE in my SHOE

Something's Broken

You think you will get used to
the accumulation of loss,
(your spine, left hand, right foot,
twisted ribs), but your asymmetry
sharpens, crooks. Something's
broken inside: a sharp razor blade
rattling about, a loose screw,
a wire crossed. The on switch
turns everything off. You can
hammer your hand,
feel nothing. Pain circuits require
repair; you require repair.
Behold the transformation.
You coin yourself: Electrician of My Body.
Order the tool belt, manuals, supplies.
A body rebuilt is a monster better. This
time, you'll max that village out.

Twisted

The surgeon has straightened
    me out as best he can, my bones
        fused, twined with stainless steel.

Pins harness my skittish vertebrae,
    ball bearings support my questionable
        spine, my sideways being.

I am myself, but a new construction,
    too. People treat you different
        when you are no longer bent.

I see it in their face, the absence
    of dismissal. The lack of quick
        and fulsome pity, the small smile.

I fear my spine, leaning, listing,
    going slant again. I fear the return
        to what I was. I have become an expert

on curvature. I've learned a world of new terms,
    acquired fluency in deformity's language.
        Kyphosis. Stenosis. Scoliosis.

Hunchback. Call my misshape what you will. I could say
    that's gone, the titanium rods are all
        inside, crooked is my secret.

But one can only hide so much. The defects are always there,
    like the flaws in a weakened bridge,
        the mending plates in a rehabbed house.

Straight's been way overrated; the cripple lurks
    inside. And she comes out, whenever there's
        something I don't like. I tilt,

I stumble, I shuffle down the corridors. I remind
    you of what you're not. I shoulder myself
        against walls. I keep the center off.

Love Letter to My Surgeon

There I am on my side,
        a trussed pig, a slab of meat,
dressed for incision, and invasion.

I'm cleaned and shaved,
        sterilized and almost naked
on the gleaming silver table.

There is always so much metal.
        Everything cold, bright,
appliance, in this arena.

I squint and wait for meds.
        The music's loud,
aggressively happy,

as the nurses will be soon.
        I am the only one naked,
or almost naked. There's a wisp

of a hospital gown draped over me.
        You think I don't notice,
spread-eagled on the table,

but I do. I always watch
        until the last possible moment
when right before I go under,

you walk in like a rock star.
        You become attention's center.
I, object on the table. Prepped.

Chit-chat felt necessary.
        Let's have a party.
Don't mind me—you've a free

pass to this body.
        Love my liver, admire
my spleen, stare at the intestines.

So much. You aren't
        the first;
you won't be the last.

I invite you, I am letting you
        get this close,
inside me, veins, arteries,

and finally, jackpot,
        my crooked spine,
because you said you could

fix me, promised. Or it seemed
        you implied repair, renewal.
Why else would I let you swim

in my flesh, when I'm more under
          than a six whiskey
bender. It's like love.

You touched me tenderly, Doctor,
          with your witty surgical
hats and masks.

I wasn't just some pig, carcass
          split open for business.
I was a beloved, a wife, a daughter.

Your fingers were so delicate,
          I have to think. My spine,
in that moment, unlike any other.

The Hour of the Raccoon

In the hour of the raccoon, sharp claws
savage my ducks, one by one.
Claws scrape their feathers, teeth
tear their flesh. Once they find
your fowl, they settle in; they go for the rest.
But maybe it wasn't them.
Weasel. Dog. Snake. Coyote. Human.
Death is all over the farm this week.
The bay horse dropped in the field,
his tan partner won't stop whinnying
for him to *come back come back.*
The tabby kitten crawled the wrong
way, now her spine's broken, unhinged.
Five chickens had their throats slit
by something other than me.
Autumn's starting to gnaw; the night
air dampers. Pepper calls for Bucky,
follows us down to the corpse, which is
and is not, Bucky, his one other.
We should *do something, do something.*
Pepper neighs all night. His body crashes
through brush and branches. *Bring me
back mine.* I can't bring any of them back.
Not my sister. Not my mother. Not the animals.

The Good, Good Cripple

The good, good cripple does not slow
the group with her hitched gait.
That drag foot knows its place:
close to the margin marked
accommodation.

If she insists on trying to hike,
swim, bike, she must acknowledge
the disadvantage becomes.
Warn the leader ahead of time.
When she does, all smile
their small smile. Waste and wait.
Perfume hides her Poise pad stench.
Expensive, baggy clothes cover
her kyphosis.

Fuck the good, good freak.
There's Travel TV, National Geo, PBS.
No more struggle to navigate unknown
steps, gone the soiled, extra bathroom
minutes. Why not leave The Group?
Strike out on a different path,
like the one ahead. Already
she's wandered on—where weeds,
mushrooms, belladonna,
and hemlock flourish.

I pick a devil's walking stick;
Balance is a fickle bitch—she comes,
then goes. One fox, two does, four hawks;
one owl ignores my stumbling. No one
calls my name. Soon return won't work.
Bluebells, then black, unidentified snakes:
I'm out deep. *Wilderness is
wilderness.* Beauty; danger.
Calculated risk.

Ahead there will be a bluff,
riddled with undergrowth trees.
Exposed roots twine, work to
break free. Choosing time. One
step down: brokenness. One
step up: pain, inability, and
unending loss.

My Last Poem

I am the perfect poem; so well-behaved.
Look at how my lines line up,
a gentle, even path through the forest.
My tone's cultivated, gently assertive.
I do not want to startle the reader.
No sudden bloated opossum corpses
lurk around the corner, no stumble
into tangled thickets, chiggers,
thorns. No strange rashes or itches,
just a gentle stroll—*until...*
of course, there's an until,
there always is. Sudden wind.
A drop in temperature.
Lightning strikes have been
detected 2.1 miles from this poem.
Take shelter. Lightning strikes now
detected .1 miles from this poem.
Severe weather pinpointed
exactly where you are.
Hail breaks through the stanza's
canopy. A wind shear carries
off your best thoughts. A mistake
has been made. Fatal errors have
occurred. There is too much
muchness in these woods.
Time to bushwhack your way
out. Poison ivy, ticks, copperheads.
No matter. They are you. This is
what you grew up with;
this is what you know.

A fellow hiker shouts over
the gale: *you appear to be struggling.*
Perhaps you should turn back.
To what? The melancholy of my bed,
the nursing of failing limbs,
the encroaching immobility,
a pillar of salt. Give me
what you've got. In this poem,
I will walk until I fall,
I will crawl on all fours
until I expire. I will
go out as I came in.
Naked. Howling. Hole.

The Burning Girl

On the family farm we used all
the flammables. Kerosene. Gasoline. Diesel.
I could light each, with a quick, an expert touch.
I knew how to scorch and burn.
I knew how high, how low to let
the fire burn. Garbage cans.
Brush piles. Leaves. Fallow fields.
Abandoned houses. Old tires.
Dead cows. Each one had a different look.
Each one had a different smell. I
learned to clean the messes up.
I learned to shovel ash, gray powder,
black, flakes, ruined stumps, melted
rubber, charred bones. I swept up.

Of course, my mother wanted
cremation. We knew fire so well.
Her ashes smudged all over me.
With one breeze, a fire can shift,
take a deadly, unexpected turn.
The summer leaves shifted;
she blew into my eyes, my nose,
my hair. The cancer burned
nothing now.

I am so tired of tending fires. This poem
scares me--because I am uttering
the unsaid: this will most likely
be my fate as well. I have the same
cells, I share her repressed genes.
The multiplication may have already started,
the burning running through my bones.
Another fire, another death.
I prepare for my cremation.
I swear I see the smoldering.
Unless, of course, I'm wrong.
Fires are so fucking tricky.

The Princess and the Pea

I opened the window, started throwing
   things out. Goodbye love, so long typewriter, flowered
     flounce chair, whiskey tumbler,
        full ashtray, unsmoked cigarettes.

There goes ambition, bounce,
   bounce. Next comes love, the pink and red
     starred quilt, the delicately stitched moon patterns.
        No more having to lie in what I've made.

I keep looking for that tiny pea of disturbance,
   that one word if erased, whited out, rephrased,
     would let me rest. But nothing comes; I am blankness.
        Cover my wounds; shroud my sorrows.

Out go the photos, out goes the phone, out all
   the maimed writings that refuse to add up.
     Soon it will be me flying through the window. Down,
        down goes the princess. How did I

get this so wrong? I just wanted a little quiet
   rest. A pea safe inside a pod. I wanted to crawl
     down deep into the heart of everything, a seed snug
        in layered dirt. I wanted the world to cushion me,

like layers and layers of inflatable bedding. I wanted
   Costco sized security. No wonder it was never
     enough. The entire world is my disturbance—niggling,
        needling, the stone in my shoe.

The Winter of the Duck

The three ducks left call.
They won't alone. Then two.
Then only the male who diligently
watches the iced corpse of his beloved.
For three days, I try sticks, rocks, calling,
on sheer ice. Nothing.
I've failed. A blizzard eats
the pond, my heart: *there* he is—
cowered under his pen.
Put me back. For six days, he won't
move, for five he won't eat.
On the sixth, he pecks, then scarfs his corn;
Oh the black round his golden pupil:
how we wounded long for spring.

Churchill

This should have been a poem about going
to Canada with my sister, about seeing
polar bears for the first time with her.

Should, should, should. But she died.
So in this poem I go without her to Churchill
where the cold rises, a snap that stings.

My memories of her condense, to a heavy
point within my chest, a hot white light.
Outside there is the crush of snow, glare of ice—

wood smoke clings to coat, hat, gloves, skin.
The landscape here bleeds white, barren.
Bah. I don't have the patience for this.

I want to remember *more,*
but the details slip. How did she
hold her head when she told that joke?

I'm sure my tour group became politely,
patiently bored with my stories.
All that ice could not numb.

I talked, and talked, and talked
until one of the guides reminded me
that my loss is not the only one.

Listen. This is a story he told me. A woman
in the final stages of MS desires to see
a polar bear before she dies.

Her mobility is limited, her senses shutting down—
and yet stubbornly she insists this is
what she will live to see.

How precise, how exact that wish.
How precise, how exact all our final wishes
—perhaps that is the most

we may hope for: a certain specificity—
something that can be both
understood and fulfilled,

a polar bear scuffing across the ice,
scruffy symbol, image
for all one has lost.

Self-portrait/Burn

After your sister dies,
you feel scorched, hollow,
the shell of a burnt out house.
A controlled fire. You knew
it was coming.

The metaphors continue: you
see yourself as split, an apple sliced
neatly down the core, a blue glazed plate,
carelessly dropped, cleaved in two.
A twig snapped. A broken match.

The person before your sister
died, and the one after. Look, two girls
in a July haze of cornfield, two
girls in a beat-up Pontiac, driving
through Iowa, two girls in a pasture.

Two girls warming by a crackling
bonfire. Then there's one
stuck with the rest of the story.
A green clothesline strung across
an empty lawn. A sad blue chair.

A worn down red lighter. The loneliness of
unmatched things. Driving through Iowa,
you smoked cheap cigarettes because what
did it matter: she was already dying, the
summer was already blazing.

You get up. You breathe in and out. You
give up a hundred times, offer anything
to keep her here. Nothing will in the end.
The metaphors accumulate, catch fire, flame.
You are left with her cattle, chewing their cud.

Her pale orange cat on a bamboo
floor. The sun moves, and he's
gone. The world weighs so heavy,
and then, without notice, so light.
We end, always. We smolder, singe.

Bring it on. Burn down this lovely life.
Your heart will break again,
but not in the same way--
so fully, so completely,
so brutally in two--
one half into memory,
one half into calcified pain.

The Worrying Hour

It is the hour of dread, when anxiety grips
    my heart and wrings it like a pink rubber sponge.
I pump fear so well, the supply doubles.
    Soon the national gross product will triple.
I've flooded the market, lowered the price,
    devalued the product. The sky is falling.

The weathers are changing. The tornados
    are meaner; the thunderstorms belligerent.
Snakes race in black and blue weathers.
    The whole world's alarm system seems
to be off. Danger, danger, Will Robinson.
    There's no going back. Not in this hour.

In this hour, worry rules. It breathes the air for me; it slithers
    like a thick black snake coiled right
on my bed. A huge vulture shadowing my days,
    a heavy ash smoke rolling towards the window.
My mother, dying, saying, let's get this over with.
    The helplessness of that hour. When all

I can do is lie down and wrap the ragged terror around my limbs,
    a thick mourning cloth. There is no way out.
This hour wears me like a coal gray sack. I know my father
    will die, too. I run through all the possible deaths.
It will be the one I forget to name. On high alert,
    I go into a frequency beyond myself.

My soul quivers. My body tremors. The snake hisses, lengthens.
    The smoke envelopes my head. Dark wings brush my face.
My heart races to escape, my mind blank as a faceless clock.
    My life ticks in this hour's hold. The parameters
are strong, and strict. I must believe in *before* and *after*.
    I must believe this is only allotment, a brutal unit measured.

Grading on a Late Winter Day

I am grading; it's getting late
   in the day. Crow's feet gather on my face.
     Brown dots speckle my hands.
        This is what I do; this is what I've been doing
           for a long time. Cornfields, snow and ice.

The wind here howls like a siren at midnight,
   the kind that screeches through a small farm town,
     down the lonely, boarded up main street, past
        the water tower, the topless silo, the cemetery,
           the dead's' cold bones, down the hard road,

asphalt cracking, potholes growing,
   down into a soft wail, fading into the slush
     from the last February sleet.
        The bay of the frustrated, the cry of the
           trapped. I once howled like that, but now

I keep quiet. My days of loud are over. My ears
   muffled, my eyes watery. But I hear
     my students. Their voices rise,
        ragged, rough, harsh, growling, shuffling,
          from their essays' pages. It's a rumbling,

then a roar. All that need and want rising like a Spring
   flood, getting ready to break, to cut flat loose,
     and run for the farthest corners of this earth,
        where they will try to carve their names. Maybe one
          or two will manage an escape from this dirt, this world.

And the rest will fall into a steady silence. The silence of recliners
   and beers. The silence of mid-life. The silence of endings.
     The silence that pushes on us all. I have been doing this
        for a long time, and they keep coming. Their voices
          might save even the quietest of us.

A Bargaining with my Forest's Fox

Red fox, kill or kit in your teeth,
you move so you are always just
on vision's edge---trotting towards
the trees. You sense how much
I want to see you, you sense
my damned domestication.
We both know it's wrong.
A major mistake occurred in my making.
Red fox: I need to be you—bones and muscle
draped with ragged fur, savage pointed teeth,
impeccable ears, light foot.
Scent. Pulse. Blood lust.
The place I work might miss
the switch. No more remediation,
obedience training. Their written reprimands,
crumpled, scat-smeared could waft
away, white birds in wind.
Like doves. A pair. To tame
the female of a species,
corner, maim, or kill her mate.
She'll lose her footing, circle back Confused. She'll whine,
paw the ground.

In my office, I jiggle the mouse
uselessly. Authorities, once trusted,
have fired my husband. My office chair
spins me. The walls close in.
We'll both turn animal now,
flee into poverty. As for the students,
we'll leave one letter—boldly
printed, taped to a bathroom door:
Do not trust your education. Instinct
bears better results. Assess the data.
Run the numbers. Sniff the wind.
If you catch the reek of disaster,
if your eyes tear from burning debt,
if you are told to remain calm,
you are already in the storm's eye.
You've become the bottom line.
Already spent. All mythologies
point to this: never trust one holding
a ledger, an arrow, a gun. Gods will be gods.
Cruel, vengeful. Bored.
Often dumb. Howl all you want.

No one will listen, except those
in the forest, ready for the wounded,
and their bright
blood trail.

After My Banishment

You didn't really think I was gone
that easily, did you? Everyone knows
the monster never truly dies.
Maybe I melted into a puddle, or burst
into flames, maybe I wandered toward
the horizon while signing goodbye.
I heard your repressed sighs of relief.
I'd hardly shuffled from the frame.
Yet there you gather.
All good monsters know huddles
invite revenge. Each person turns their back—
why I could snap your neck before
The Next Step. You need a new fear.
You need Someone to point
The Finger of Not One of Us toward.
There are two thing Authority fears most:
resistance and curiosity. When that poor,
reanimated corpse questioned
his maker, I felt a sharp pain.

We beasts know our place; you'd die
without us. Who would give you
the insolent arch of a black wing;
the determined uttering no. Bellow.
Roar. Rage. My gimped feet shuffle
leftward, crows close behind.
A strange shape in restless shadows.
I need you as much as you need me.
Without purpose, I vanish. Of course,
since we don't exist, (monsters never do),
I do as I please: change into your favorite
daughter, your mother, stalk your day.
At night, I turn faceted mirror, and reflect
your deepest nightmares:
your image, my face.

The Bad Girl

In sixth grade, we got in
trouble for something.
Don't ask me what.

The other girls cried, quivered,
promised they'd never
do it again.

Their punishment: lines
of apologetic text. I sneered:
quicker option, please.

Paddle me hard, spank me fast.
The principal hefted his big
oak plank down.

Did you think I'd go the safer route?
Patience pained me,
just punish already.

Next things contained better
intrigue: broken boys,
whiskey bottles, back seats.

Muscled and mad, I knew how
to jump into fire, get shit over.
I'd push my hand through

glass; slam against ground.
Pound dirt. Life came fast, a Spring
flood. No time for interruptions.

Beat me, chastise me,
correct me, but don't detain me.
I bent my little girl butt over marking

the beginning of many bending-overs.
Eyes half-open. Thoughts erased.
Body poised and tense.

Acquiring the art of faked acquiescence, I became
a sly container, one shameless receptacle.
Butter won't melt in this mouth.

Little Red 2.0

Yeah, the wolf was real, but
that doesn't make the story less
stupid, and, frankly, so familiar—
there're LOTS others like it.
I'm just a rip off of a facsimile of
a copycat. A dime a dozen
in .99 cent dvd barrel.

Oh, I would've liked a tale with some
thing different, something fast and racy.
One where I didn't have to traipse.
I've always loathed that word.
The wolf, let me tell you, was so
scratchy, smelly, beyond annoying,
but I rubbed his balls, he purred.

No matter how far ahead I read,
I couldn't get out. Somebody made
sure of that. The ending was sealed
tight as a princess' legs. So
I started stockpiling guns
and ammo as best I could. The mall
down the lane ran specials.

If you look closely at a text,
you can almost always find a loophole.
I did. One where I could wiggle
my little trigger finger through.
Step one: take out the beast.
Step two: figure out what
will take its place.

Step three: prep for the reporters.
How does freedom taste?
A long tall blonde news jockey
leans particularly close. Just like I thought:
sharp and salty, with filaments of honey,
juicy heart, racy elbows, unending hair.
The wolf in me can't get enough.

The Feral Child

When they crammed me into clothes,
dropped me at the school, unceremoniously,
with all the other little beasts. I knew
the jig was up. I knew this wasn't
going to go down well.

Doesn't play nice with others. Has trouble sharing.
Poor understanding of boundaries.
Oh, I understood boundaries alright.
There was my space in this world.
Then there was everyone else.

Rules were everywhere. Unwelcome.
Forbidding. Confusing. Of course,
I bared my teeth and snarled. Who wouldn't?
I pissed in the corner. I picked
my nose. I knew some basic shit

outside of books. Like: bare back's best,
hound dogs share their ticks, and following
the low snake creek will almost always
get you home. Yeah, my mama,

with her own sharp teeth, wild eyes,
warned me about this world. Dirt
in my nails, fleas on my arms, bramble
hair, I loved: rolling in dust, pond wallowing,
skunk mud, high oaks, callused feet.

I feared: speakers, schedules, sitting
still. Shut windows. Closed doors.
How was I supposed to breathe?
The axis of the world had shifted.
My mama instructed me: the exits

are few, and far between. Park
yourself next to one. Wait
for your chance, and then,
run, darling,
run.

Childhood of the Storyteller

Story One.
When I was seven, I told
my mother the kids at school
called me names, pushed frogs
in my face, made me put my lips
on the soft, amphibious skin.

Story Two.
I was an awkward child.
They did things. I placed my
version in gravel lots' dark corners—not
the locker room's showers.

Story Three.
I spelled out my suffering in forked
tongue; I hissed and croaked.
The playground was a monstrosity.
I crawled into my reptile skin; I slid
into the swamp.

Revision.
My parents and teachers
wondered what was wrong.
Why couldn't I tell the truth?
I twisted my hands.

Story Four.
Toad.

Story Five.
For show and tell, I opened my palm:
See this polished stone; it turns you to something Other.
Our second chance.
They washed my mouth out
with soap, set me in the corner—
red chair on black and white
linoleum squares. Liar, liar,
pants on fire.

Next.
Memory will cover the mess;
you tell yourself what you need to.
I was a lovely child. I had lots of friends.

The Truth.
What they lacked in imagination,
they made up for with fists.
My nose bent, broke. My mouth
burbled blood and spit. Every
crowd needs a scapegoat.
We hold the group together.
Why me?—One of childhood's oldest
stories. I made do with what I had.
I leaned into the words;
I bit down hard.

How to Save Your Self

First you must pack up all
your madnesses, from noon's pink
nightgown to evening's vulnerable confusions,
from the green silk of drink and pills,
to fear's dark black compulsions. Shove
their angry coils into a sturdy army surplus bag,
slide its zippered teeth shut on the banging
of your lost souls.

They'll escape, they always do.
So ignore them when they intrude
on your ordered days. Keep your face calm
as a swollen lake, a placid mirror, a surface
that hides so much. They will rise through
the bamboo floor, seat themselves in the oak
dining chairs. They'll bang against the stovepipe,
a trapped starling frantically trying to get out,
they'll pummel the door like a frustrated child,
they'll wail, You think you're free? You think
the wind outside is a mild breeze?

Focus on the coming storm. Notice
the drops of rain already spattering.
You'll have to move quickly,
you'll have to decide who to save.
You can't keep hoarding them; you
can't keep loving them. You must
go to the basement, find the room
with the treasured candlesticks,
the generations of photos, your cow
figurines, your treasures,
and your duffel bag.

Carry it to the pond behind the house,
wait until the last of the summer geese
has left, listen for the evening killdeer,
watch for the yellow black belly of this
year's water snake, and when the bullfrogs
start their mournful bellow, and the fireflies
began their luminescence, you must drown
all but one. Choose carefully
which madness you keep
for it will be the only one
you have to battle loneliness, to walk
with late at night when the full moon hangs
so heavy, when your heart is tired,
when you want some reminder
of all that raged within.

Beating the Boundaries

        You have asked and asked again,
beating nightly at my door. Clenched
fist, raised hand, questioning, insistent—
        Why did I leave? Look at my eyes:
corn-yellow, barn-brown, irises shot
through with dust. How can you believe
        I've succeeded? In this city I exhale
your landscape, my breath misty and fogged, hair
tangled, a bale of hay. I've left, and I've
        left myself behind.

        My great-grandfather slammed my
grandfather's palms against the farm's
border: rock, oak, post—slammed until his
        blood smeared across barren stone, seeped
into old wood. Three months for his hands
to heal. My fingers are calloused,
        lightly, at the tips. Still, I've memorized: This
is the northwest corner, the granite rock.
This is the southwest, the upright row of
        devil's walking sticks.

        In sleep I walk deep in your
interior where pollen drifts
like rain, and creeks swirl with the quick silver
        tails of minnows. I step into
your rivers, your limerock streams, clay banks.
Who says geography is the soul?
        I know the answer: each time returning,
I return with nothing more than the dust
in a drowned man's pockets. I am that dust,
        scattering, then lost.

Envelope

To enclose, to hold, to wrap
around. To cradle delicately, gently,
securely. To seal for safe transport,
to shelter the message, the words
sent far away, where they would travel
for days, through the post offices of Champaign,
and Carbondale, and Des Moines, bumping
in the back of dusty trucks, falling
away from our fingers, full
of intent. Submissions sent to the west,
and the east, to the editors, to the journals,
to those cities we had read of.
How we believed in sending the message,
loudly and hopefully, into the big,
bigger beyond us. Such dreams
penned in those writings. Our landscape
one of envelopes, and typewriters, and stamps,
and return address ink pads.
How we tried to speed it all up,
now we long for the slowing down,
so typical. The nostalgia, the remembrance,
the loving only after it is gone.
The image of my lonely typewriter in the plane's
overhead compartment—its keys hot
with those early poems of love,
and escape.

Those That Come Back

We are uneventful here, we who have returned:
the dutiful, the wounded, the living, the good,
the adult child. You may call us
by different names, but identify us
by the depth, the strength of our return.
Now back, we are forever here,
as rooted as the oaks and pines.
You can tell us by our patience,
the long lines of waiting in our face,
the settled air around us, the settled dust
within our homes. You can tell us
by our affinity for the winter night,
whose muffled layers soothe our memories
of other lives. We love the glazed, still
surfaces of our backfield ponds.
And yet, we try to make life
happen, to break this thick block ice
insulating us, but all we get are sharp rib pains,
labored breath, billowing across
the frozen fields.

Shades of summer birds haunt the pond;
their shadows brush the ghosts of former lives,
selves we buried so relentlessly. They've dug
themselves up, and dance just out of reach—
mocking... All that you could have been...

The other dead faded dreams would gather,
if they could, but they are trapped
still in their dank burial boxes,
weighted by sadness, love. Patiently,
they suffocate beneath the layers
of perpetual snow. So much lost along the way.
So much accepted, so much ground
down with the season. The drying husks,
the composting. Fat black tadpoles move
sluggishly below the pond's ice. My life
barely moves within these bundled layers.
The years accumulate. The woodpile grows.
This winter bears down on us all.
Our houses weaken, the rafters shift,
mice grow bold in the hallways and shower,
the paint peels, and the windows loosen.

And, oh, how our parents dwindle.
They are beginning to look like distant
children, peering at the brutal landscape
fast approaching. Their tracks in the snow
grow lighter, footprints
smudged and rising.

Days of 1979

When we slid into her dad's four by four,
we were smart as anything. Slim,
long-limbed, we oiled our bodies
as much as the truck—hands lingering
over each curve, fender, each slender hip.
Camels, unfiltered, were the only things
we'd smoke, flicking the ashes, then our hair,
blown the color of hay dried and raked
all summer. She shifted gears,
grinding from first to fourth,
pushing the polished red Ford forward,
an eight horse engine out of the gate,
revving past the Bar-B-Que, the Sunoco,
and onto the two-lane highway, running
from town. In those days of 1979,
we were racing toward the lives we knew
existed somewhere beyond the cornfield's horizon,
beyond the dust, beyond our town's dimming lights.
At night, we would ignite with whiskey,

rock n' roll, and boys on the seat.
She always said, the faster we drove,
the better it got, until the familiar oaks,
wheat, corn, bluebells and sweet williams finally dropped
away. Her lips red, her nails pale enameled pink,
she talked of skyscrapers, elevators, neon signs,
of the way the nights stayed bright in a city—-
as if we could see cities, as if we knew
what lives those cities might hold.
We hardly knew of death or the absences
that solidify into endless presences.
Our lives were all flux, rapid as a wild fire--
lost in the illumination, we never guessed
that those days of beginnings were also
days of endings; and I never dreamed
that her lips, her cat-green eyes, ponytailed hair,
her hands tapping the vinyl steering wheel,
would be the loss that sleeps
beside me nightly.

Mirror, Mirror

If you had to reflect princesses
all day long, you'd get tired, too.
Go ahead, they simper, tell me
I'm the fairest, the grandest,
the prize. Always, I whisper,
you wash in the looks of men,
towel dry with the leftovers.
That prince never stood a chance.
Valiant, Magnificent, Harry, Handsome,
Dick; all the same. I get weary. My words,
never enough. These girls want more.
Silvered reflection, shadowed truths.
I cast their beauty back at them—
their breasts, lips, hips, cheeks still plump
as the orchard's freshest peach.
Later comes the drying out, the collapse.
Wrinkles, sags, erasure.
And then, dear girls,

nothing will save you. No mud tinctures,
pharmacy grade ointments, holy water, snake oil,
botox or filler will stop the desiccation.
Then you'll break me into thirteen jagged pieces,
but each shard will still tell a tale: once upon a time,
this princess was beauty, now she is revelation.
Am I the wickedest? Look into my tarnished eyes.
I was you; I paid the price. Every girl has to.
The-it-can't-happen becomes the-happened,
age's impossible black shoe squarely on one's foot.
Here, on the other side, we become something
different, crone-shaped and powerful. The blue skies
no longer thrill us, we want storms descending.
Winter's cold winds, the loss of permanence—
oh, we plan to sing and dance in the subtraction.
With each loss we grow, until finally, we are nothing,
and everything—the sum at the end,
the sheet covered mirror.

How to Leave Yourself

1

Wait until the day rubs against you
like transparent silk and your skin
feels as smooth as an extended nap,
the only disturbance the coming dusk.

Stare at the diminished light, the place
where orange sky sinks into field.
Walk to that exact spot and step
through, not as though entering water,

but cautiously climbing—
right leg followed by left
as though lifting yourself over the last
electric fence.

2

Whatever you do, don't look back.
The wheat shimmers in the moonlight;
the rustling of the elms' leaves
sound out your name.

It's so much easier
than you ever would have guessed.
Behind you the shadows of a girl with raven hair
sink into mud, manure, cornfields, dust.

3

What you walk toward is vaster
than the solar system and smaller
than a single pore upon your body.
What you walk toward reeks with a honeysuckle

scent. It's as tall and persistent
as the Johnson grass you once knew.
It's as dizzying as the top of the tallest
white oak, shaking in lightning storm's wind.

It is the culmination of every night
slept beneath a red-starred quilt—
dreaming of the rutted paths the cows take
when they never come home.

Vow Vigilance

I know the going, not the staying–
I like to take my leaving quick.
I live for unpaid rent, dented friendships,
boredom, lust, lost bills, misplaced keys.
Time to pack my plaques, my books,
my sack of family photos. Goodbyes jar—
sad ritual of hugs, kisses, see you soon.
So I go: cat out window, snake under door,
ghost, whisper, flee. Motion masters me.
One minute I'm there, the next—breeze,
face in mirror, brief memory. I know
the roads of loaded car, midnight drives.
Asphalt gives to corn. I go to find
myself, I go to leave myself. I go
before some lover, friend, or boss
finds the path that splits my brain–
packed dirt lined with weeping willows.
My sister hikes ahead. Some going
times I see her near a bend. I race,
but she runs faster, toward our mother.
I must bargain a return. Vow vigilance.
Swear to find the bio markers, scan all
systems, terrorize the answer holders,
gain admittance to working trials.
Break the code, find the first lump,
smaller than a pea. Then, I'd see
the Signs before they started signing.
Before their crosshairs sighted me.
Before mutation, before my going.
Before departure equals gone.

Fairytale

She cocks her head with its long brown
hair, and talks down to me.
She's like an ice queen, a princess.
In my house.

The world revolves around her.
I am humbled by my new
insignificance. My minor role
in this tale.

I provide shelter, food,
I provide something to ignore.
While wolves didn't leave her
at my door, they might as well

have for all the affinity she has
for me. The mammal smell I emit is faintly
musky. We both scent female.
We both use our mouth to eat.

Here the similarities end. She's
in this story because she has to be.
Until she finds her exit
which she's steadily sniffing for.

I didn't bring her into this world,
but I still feel guilt. She
doesn't care how she got here,
what it took. What she would like

is Out. And my middle aged body
is so blocking the way. She'll
study me, she'll watch how
I maneuver. And then she'll

mimic my words, my tone,
my clothes, my gifts.
She's a brilliant impostor.
All survivors are.
Like me. When they brought me in,
I was bloodied and torn.
I might be her mother.
Or the hag with the apple.

And what about love?
If we could just insert a red
thread of warmth, a yellow
strand of care, then we might
have a better story. One that
doesn't have to end

with the body in the well.
One that opens in a new direction.
I fed her milk. I warmed her
hands. Death went to
a different door.

My Place in Line

Our seasons change swiftly.
Sudden silence of insects.
Cattle bedding before sundown.
Finches, cardinals, sparrows fatten;
start hanging by my window for seed.
The hummingbirds leave all at once.
There on Monday, Tuesday gone.
No bird gets left behind. My sister
starts falling apart first, mother follows
close. I know the signs; I see
the shortened breaths, longer naps.
Their eyes hurt me most: each time,
there's a fatigue like departure. A hand
waving good-bye from a car, an airplane,
life's bus.

Through winter, I scramble, try to hold
their bodies together. Chemo. Mouth balms. IVs.
Tamoxifen, Hep-era, ports, steroids, narcotics.
I scour the Internet. Bible of doom and gloom.
The message clear: lie down now; it's over;
we're sorry; give up. I don't.
Of course, I am left behind.

What we do doesn't save us.
Or anyone else. Departure's
already occurring. Listen:
diminishment. The dying
have more important things
to attend to: like dying.
Grief is their nation,
I'll have my chance later.
When the hummingbirds return,
I greet them by myself.
Put food in their feeder.
Line-cutting not allowed here.
Gravestones set up chronologically.
I have my marker, position.
The one unfinished headstone.
Death date: Incomplete.

Broken Things

It had been a long time since she had been outside. Everything was different. Crumpled metal that had once been a tool she couldn't identify, one her husband had held skillfully in his hands, the gleaming tool throwing dirt everywhere, now was twisted, broken, almost beyond recognition. She'd never asked its name. There were many things she had never asked. He loved to talk, or had, and she loved to listen. Two steps took her to the bottom of a shovel, its wooden handle snapped neatly in two. Under the porch, she saw what she could only make out as shapes of things—objects scrambled together.

There is a sliver of ice that shoots through the veins when one realizes things are not what they seemed. She loved her husband, trusted her husband, placed a kind of faith in him. It made no sense–what she was seeing. Her feet felt very light as if she were drifting off, then a moment later: leaden. She continued walking. A trail of black and red feathers led to the corpses of seven chickens, their throats all neatly, cleanly slit. The blood upon their necks had dried, but how long ago, she did not know. She looked to her right: red clay flower pot shards littered the ground. What was once a garden had been destroyed, roots up where they shouldn't be. Their concrete sidewalk had been busted open. Several trees were down.

In the pit of her stomach, a small ball of regret formed; there was evidence of a voluminous anger everywhere. How long since she had been outside? Days, weeks, months? Her nightgown swayed around her ankles. This might not be a safe place to be. She felt to see if she had ropes around her wrists. She did not. But she could see red, raw marks.

In the distance was the outline of a man. His shoulders were broad, like her husband's. He rhythmically swung an axe, down, then up, then down. There was a fury in his movements. She should not be out here. But still she watched the rise and fall of the axe. He was, and wasn't her husband. She was, and wasn't herself. She was sorry she had failed; she was so sorry she angered him so. She should go back, before he saw her.

A wind whipped up as she turned. Her nightgown swirled, billowed; the blue cloth wrapped around her ankles, suddenly tight. So much betrayal everywhere, she thought–even in the silk of her sleepwear. She tried to fall as quietly as possible, she tried to lean away from his direction. She tried to meet the ground gently. Everything would end at some point. Perhaps the sooner, the better. When her head hit, it hit solidly, and a blessed black blankness filled her mind.

In Reseda

The sky is ugly today,
dead gray. The ocean smells
of trash, and fish. In Reseda,
in the unfamiliar foreign
waters of LA, a young woman
I knew from treatment
has died. I'm more angry
than anger can do. I'm so tired
of this. The sudden loss,
the overdose, then the gone.
This world's an ugly place,
and it seems its young are dying
sordid deaths. The allure
of coming back from death's
edge, the glorious feel,
the lure of Fentanyl. I am caught
between being and not. I am
caught on a barbed hook
baited with the shame
of I am not dead. The times
I have woken, thought this,
seem too many to count.
The relief that instantly
floats in my chest,
the not me inhale,
then the grief and guilt.

This becomes a way
of living, this becomes
California for me. Everyone
I learn to love in treatment
carries within them both
death and hope. Two sides
to a west coast coin.
Fate flips like
a caught fish,
followed by a reeling
in, and then either
the throwing back
to live again,
or not.

The Good Girl

I was a good girl. All fluff,
and soft, and full of too many
ways. Such a good girl that they locked
me up, and threw away the keycard,
erased the access code, blocked
my phone number. Except
on Fridays, those zombie afternoons,
when visitors arrived. More candy,
more chocolate, more diet
coke, please. Cigarettes
really hit the mark. I was
so good at being good,
I cracked and fell apart. Oh no
here comes the crystal chandelier,
tinkle, tinkle, shatter into
a hot lot little pieces of bad.
The bad was so big, it got
everywhere. In my eyes, in my
mouth, in my heart and hair. What
I wanted most was: love.
What I wanted, second most:
to be left alone, like a cat hidden
in a box. And third-most, to never
be left alone. Find me, find me,
find me, please. The nurses, kind,
kept offering up structure. The doctors,

also kind, pills. I took both, and
travelled further from the bad,
and the good. I travelled until
I couldn't remember my name,
or my reasons. This was
very good for me. So good,
I broke again, like a tidal wave,
a tsunami against a hard dirt shore.
The water went everywhere. I went
everywhere. A brilliant fluid mess
they couldn't begin to mop up.
And so they gave me a new room.
One with more restrictions.
This time, I hardened
into a cube. A saucy little square.
A brick. A block. You could
make something with this;
build something on it.
I knew better than to shatter again.
I learned to love this form. This
firmness. What I'm saying is:
I learned my place. I learned
how to hold my hands,
folded, in my lap, just so.
I learned to be contained. Watch me:
Behave. Behave. Behave.

Recipe for Disaster

First, stop cooking.
Let all the domesticity
of your lovely kitchen
wither. Let mold fill the fridge,
dishes pile in sink.
Let the roaches gather.

The tidying of pillows,
pictures, books, schedules,
and, yes, writing, forgotten.
Weeds blossom. You're a wild
field now; a pasture
gone to seed.

Make a strewing powder:
lavender, peppermint, straw.
Spread on the linoleum. Still,
you can't cover despair's stench:
rotten apples, vodka, burnt
bangs, gas lit cigarettes.

Guzzle your drink. He's not
coming tonight, or tomorrow.
Your poems are rejected.
The promise you arrived with,
a white pillbox hat, matching coat,
falls off. Stop paying your bills.

What's potential, but a chance
to prove loss. Make another.
Kick your sleeping dog awake.
Break a mirror for good luck.
None of the given rules work.
You're broken, a battered cat.

Grad school's tin roof shelter
incinerated your pretty pawed feet.
Once the pet, you've doubled down
to the disaster. Heads shake
when you show up. No one warned
you: talent doesn't do disgrace.

Sleep in wadded piles of unwashed
clothes; grind your teeth at night.
Wisdom molars cut through
bleeding gums. Bare them, then witness:
you are the freak your mother
promised you'd become.

The Becoming

When a union
becomes a violence,
when a violence
becomes a brass
bed, when the bed
wears a red starred
quilt, when the quilt
becomes the pain
you rest upon,
when the dinner
plates become
fragments, when
the fragments
become shards,
when the shards
become weapons,
and the weapons
become kisses,
then the kiss becomes
lie, and lie becomes
husband, and he
becomes harm
then harm becomes
night; night, day;
day, year; year, time—
which becomes stopped,
and stopped becomes
death, while death

becomes living,
then become
is unending,
and escape
a dangerous door
that slams
and your hand quick,
yet betrays you
and your wrist weak
within bones,
then as an animal
trapped gnaws off
its snared limb,
tears muscle apart,
sever the self,
you will leave
when departing's
impossible,
let go to offer up
the violence
a hand still
holding
a doorknob,
while its body
walks a bloody
path marking
a road.

To Bring or To Not Bring Your Phone

Off to the woods, I go.
Do I bring my phone?
When first diagnosed—
the intimations of severe
pain, reduced life quality,
seemed distant as Mongolia.
I walked frequently,
often off mapped forest trails,
held my phone lightly, a minor toy.
I snapped the requisite selfie,
smiled the perfunctory smile.
When you bring your phone,
you imagine you've brought
the world. You feel you are
not alone. It thrums, trills.
At any moment, you can assess
your current state. You can
provide evidence you live.
You can see how long
before you die.
Without your phone, you might
find yourself in a tenuous
position. You might not hold
all the world's knowledge.
You would be stuck with your
own skills and tricks. Your
own reading of the sun.
You might hear your breath,
It's steady rise and fall.
A sound you have forgotten
how to listen for.

You will decide, eventually,
to leave the phone at home.
You will decide when you've
had enough of everything
the portal has to give.
Then you will walk as you
haven't walked before. Death
will be closer than Mongolia.
Death will be a destination
a year or two ahead.
You will do this, or
you won't. You are still
unsure. Sometimes a trail
takes an unexpected turn,
and you are stranded
in the midst of leaves.
At the day's end, your phone
doesn't matter; how long
you lived, irrelevant.
Only one thing is going
to count: that you
have a home to go to, that
somewhere there is a bed,
pillow, sheets. You will
tuck yourself in, or if you're
really lucky, someone
will do that for you.
You will forget what a phone
was. You will remember
your mother, you will
remember your long dead
sister. You will close
your eyes, and you will
sleep, you will sleep.

Stepdaughter

She cocks her head,
long brown locks
talk down to me.
An ice princess—
royal posture
in the House.
I provide: food, shelter,
someone to ignore.
Wolves deposited her—
soft mouth, sharp teeth—
on my step. No care
for arrival's tale,
what she must is Out.
Watch as she steadily
sniffs for latch, key, door.
My sagging form blocks.
Before the next full moon,

she'll mimic my words,
tone, clothes, limp.
Brilliant impostor.
Artful understudy.
All survivors are.
Like myself. When
hustled in, bloodied, torn,
I howled every song
they wanted. I might
be her sister. I might
be the witch. Hell,
I could crook into
a hag, poison red apple
in hand—mother's
most special,
often only,
gift.

Acknowledgments

I give tremendous gratitude and appreciation to the editors and staffs of the following publications, in which these poems—sometimes in different versions—appeared or will soon be appearing:

California Quarterly: "Churchill"

Conclave: A Journal of Character: "Twisted"

Drafthorse: A Literary Journal: "The Hour of the Raccoon," "Grading on a Late Winter Day," and "The Worrying Hour"

Five Poetry: "After My Banishment"

Gingerbread House Literary Magazine: "The Feral Child"

Grief Diaries: "The Winter of the Duck"

Heron Tree: "Self-Portrait/Burn"

Literary Orphans: "Little Red 2.0" and "The Bad Girl"

Right Hand Pointing: "Something's Broken"

Rose Red Review: "The Princess and the Pea"

Rust & Moth: "The Burning Girl"

Thank You for Swallowing: "The Good, Good Cripple"

The Dandelion Review: "Love Letter to My Surgeon"

Tuck Magazine: "A Bargaining with My Forest's Fox"

VerseWrights: "Childhood of the Storyteller"

Lucy Logsdon

Lucy M. Logsdon received her MFA in creative writing from Columbia University. She teaches English and creative writing at Southeastern Illinois College. Her poems have appeared in **Nimrod**, **Southern Poetry Review**, **Poet Lore**, **Literary Orphans**, **Gingerbread House Literary Magazine, Sixfold, Conclave, Right Hand Pointing, Thank You for Swallowing,** and **Heron Tree**.

Logsdon's poetry is often inspired by experiences she has had growing up in Southern Illinois, as well as her life as a whole.

"My work draws to some extent on my rural experiences, particularly the isolation, which always makes the rest of the world seem so odd to me," Logsdon said.

"The poems also draw, often, on my experiences as a woman grappling with the modern world. I sometimes use personas to speak the ideas of my poems."

Lucy received a **Macdowell fellowship** and has taught at **The Frost Place**. She lives in southern Illinois, raises chickens and ducks and other occasional creatures. Her outreach activities include poetry readings at local libraries and community poetry workshops.

www.ingramcontent.com/pod-product-compliance
Lightning Source LLC
Chambersburg PA
CBHW020755230426
43673CB00022B/446/J